TIME TO FIRE YOUR CUSTOMERS

Stop Letting "Customers" Run Your Business into The Ground — Focus Only On The Best Of The Best.

HUMZA CHOWDHRY

TABLE OF CONTENTS

Chapter 1
Introduction 1

Chapter 2
Are Customers Everything? 8

Chapter 3
Review Or Be Reviewed.. 16

Chapter 4
Traits And Types Of Customers 21

Chapter 5
Drawbacks Of Being Entirely Customer-Centric..................... 28

Chapter 6
Not All Money Is Good Money (Choosing Between $ And Intuition) . 33

Chapter 7
Your Engine: Employees 36

Chapter 8
Being Selective.. 39

Chapter 9
Fire Bad, Hire Good Customers... 42

Chapter 10
Off To The Races!... 47

Chapter 1

Introduction

Growing up, I never considered starting my own business. I was born in Teaneck, New Jersey, but spent most of my childhood and teenage years in the Central Valley of California. None of the people around me spoke about starting a business. However, as an elementary student, my brother and I sold countless candy bars from our backpacks to the kids at recess. We made a few hundred dollars, which we reinvested by buying more candy bars. I realized at one point that we were getting robbed by other students, who were taking candy out of our backpacks when we left for recess. Eventually, when we caught them and we reported the theft to the principal, he informed us that selling candy on school property was illegal—in fact, he shut the business down. Looking back, the candy hustle was very similar to an actual business. We had a product, an inventory system, a customer base, and real income as well as the not-so-wonderful aspects of owning a business, like theft. It was a great learning experience which would ultimately be one of my foundational roots for my desire to go into business.

Like many, I grew up in a household that was all about playing it safe. No risks. I was expected to go to school, study hard, and receive a piece of paper we call a diploma at the end of the journey. My mom always told me this piece of paper would take me places and get me a job. I do not blame her. She herself had few options available to her and wanted an easier path for her sons. As an immigrant from Pakistan, a single mother raising two young kids, I understand why she chose to play it safe rather than taking risks. It also feels good when you stay in the realm of what people expect from you. Graduating and getting degrees just felt like the norm in my family. My brother was a valedictorian with a scholarship to Berkeley. He was always ahead, smart and knew his stuff. I was nowhere near his level when it came to being book smart.

Although I was not the brightest student, I was really good at math. Math was probably my favorite subject—mainly because I was really good at it. Multiplication and division were a breeze for me; I remember when my fifth-grade teacher showed my mother how the entire class failed long division except me. That is one of my few proud academic moments. Another thing I was good at was being friendly and sociable. Growing up with very little, I learned to appreciate everything including the small things. I was easy to become friends with and relied heavily on my friends during my spare time. I spent very little time by myself.

By putting my friends first, I learned I could keep them happy and I could count on them. I remember being like a taxi driver for one of my high school friends who always needed a ride. My desire to go the extra mile for my friends was something I never personally questioned. That is... until I was unable to deliver. The time was May 2001, and I was getting ready for high school graduation. My friend requested I pick him up before heading over to graduation practice. My mom was always against the idea of taking my friends in my car, so I did not let her know I was picking my friend up. I still vividly recall the moment when we left his house, I signaled left and BAM! I was struck by an oncoming car. My world froze, my heart sank and I was in complete shock. What had just happened? How was I going to explain this to my mother? Sure enough, when my mother and brother got to the scene, I got the look of death; it was one of the saddest days I can remember. I had gone above and beyond to help a friend get to graduation practice and I ended up with a totaled car and an upset family. I ruined my brother's car, but worse, I lost my personal value as a friend. After that incident, I never heard from the friend I had been giving the ride to. He never reached out nor bothered to check in on how everything was going with me. I put my friend first and instead finished last. I lost a friend, a car, and the trust of my family. Sometimes when we put others first, we ignore the logic behind our decision making. We forget about the repercussions of our actions. And we do this in business every single day. We put customers first.

Why We Fail

We have all heard that most businesses fail within the first couple of years. This is the first thing you hear when talking with an average person about starting a business. They expect you to fail without even giving you a chance to be successful. If you think about failure without even thinking about success, your comfort zone is too narrow and small for the business world. In this book, I hope to explore and help explain that your business in the ideal sense is a paintbrush and a blank canvas. If you want to envision fear, failure, laziness and bad habits then close your eyes and paint away. However, if you have the right tools, resources and knowledge, you can carefully and strategically paint your canvas with happiness, passion, desire, impact and overcome any obstacles along the way.

If you have already started a business, ask yourself: When you decided to start your business, what was the first thought that came across your mind? How successful will my business become? How much profit will my business generate? Who will be my first customer? Being a successful business owner requires you to become a leader, lead others to share your vision, control what you can control and let go of everything else. Letting nature take its course will help prevent you from running around like a zombie trying to wear multiple hats all at once. Mastering good habits, understanding yourself and your business will help you paint your business with a fine detail brush rather than a wide and broad brush.

I do not want you to doubt your thoughts; I simply want you to let them go without giving them too much attention. While it is true that there are several hats that need to be worn when starting a business, there needs to be an understanding that you will eventually delegate these tasks once you have mastered them. I am not asking you to get every school degree in the book, but awareness leads to organizational accountability. If you simply lead the blind while being blind yourself, you will crash into everything in front of you. When you are aware and accountable, you can grow and reimagine each piece of your business. If something isn't working, lift it up, analyze it, tune it and enjoy the ride.

Business can be full of obstacles, events you can foresee – and a ton of other unforeseen ones – that we are uncertain about. Perhaps at first you envisioned a business as a side hustle, but once you're completely out of the nine-to-five routine, you wouldn't want to go back; that is, assuming you have the ideal customers.

Giving Up Not an Option

One thing to keep in mind is that as an entrepreneur, giving up is not an option. You might be starting your business right now and feeling extremely anxious and nervous about the unknowns and the uncertainties. I remember I sure was; but the path has carved itself out. You could be one or two years in, working nights and weekends, unable to take any time off and at the end only generating nominal revenues. There may be loved ones who have distanced themselves or complained about not having enough time. Remember that there is nothing wrong with being loved and being desired. Our time is limited and this world fights for our time. Whether it is binge watching a drama or perusing social media, our time is precious and critical to our lives. Use it wisely and carefully.

At this critical juncture, you'll be wondering if all your sacrifice was even worth it. But to be successful, you need to have discipline and consistency. You need to develop and master habits and routines, keeping in mind both your short term and long-term goals. These habits will help you get through your "building years" after which you will have accomplished more than most businesses ever will.

The Power of Why

You may recall going to a conference, seminar or webinar and getting high off the energy in the room. How long did that last for you? Most often it barely lasts until the next day. As humans, our attention span has been reduced to that of a goldfish. Our need and desire for rapid change in our environment does not help. With the amount of content available today it is easy to get distracted. One fundamental problem with these events, is they are not specific to your needs. It is difficult to self-analyze and be vulnerable if you lack confidence and fear being judged in front of others. If you are craving success in business, it's no surprise that you will be motivated by hearing about other business successes. The thing we are missing is personal substance and a real *Why*. Why are you here? Why are you reading this book? Why is being successful important? Why is owning a business important to you? In my opinion being successful comes down to one question: Why? If you know your whys, then nothing will stop you from getting where you want to go – not failure, distractions, people, customers, or anything or anybody else, for that matter. Your "why power" will get you up in the morning and get you to control of your life. Understand your why power – you will need it as we explore the potential customers who will attack it when you least expect it.

Chapter 2

Are Customers Everything?

When you first read the title of this book, what was your initial thought? Were you a bit surprised at the subtitle? I'll bet you were. I will be the first to let you know that customers are not everything. Yes, you heard me right. Your customers can't make or break your business. My hope is that through this book you will understand that it is YOU who are ultimately in the driver's seat. Just like when you had your idea for your business and there were naysayers telling you it was not a good idea; you will have customers who do not understand your business and will not be a good fit.

Customers are a piece of the pie, not the actual pie

To all those startups thinking they can put all of their focus on their customers and go above and beyond just to please them at all costs, stop right here and reevaluate your fundamental business strategies. Those costs can sometimes be the end of your actual business. Customers are an essential part of the way you operate your business because fulfilling their needs is what you aim to achieve, but it's not possible to provide anything and everything they might want. (That is, unless you a multi-billion-dollar industry like McDonald's, that listened to its customers and responded to their #AllDayBreakfast tweets by making their breakfast items available throughout the day and effortlessly winning the hearts of its millions of customers. The difference is that these companies are multinational and operate on a scale larger than most of our capabilities.)

Business comes first

Our goals need to be realistic and practical. Therefore, it is essential to make sure the wellbeing of your business comes first. Even before the actual physical customers. The thing with customers is – and I'm sure most of you will agree – that they will only come to you when they are requesting, demanding or expecting something from you. They do not genuinely care about your business. How many times have you finished a project or service and had a customer call in to see how the business was doing? How many times has a customer who had a not-so-great experience written a negative review on the internet? I have had my fair share of threats if I did not give in to their demands. In today's world everybody has a voice which can be posted, tweeted and shared. It is almost like being a hostage during a robbery, but you have to help the robber. The robber is in this case the customer, and your business is being robbed in front of you. You, like many business owners, are helpless.

The reality hurts

Disappointing isn't it? You feel like you did so much for a customer but got nothing return despite your efforts. Imagine the amount of time you spent on this particular customer, but it still leads to the same dead end. Disappointment. What if you were able to sort out this customer earlier, and see the red flags sooner, because you were better equipped to understand a time-killing customer? What if you realized trying to turn an unhappy person into a happy customer was simply a waste of time?

Personal Story

I am a licensed professional structural engineer, and over a decade ago, I started my own business. The year was

2009, and I still recall all the details. I had just passed my professional engineering exam and I was excited to be starting my own engineering practice. I was participating in a presentation for my network marketing business when I heard my phone vibrate. I picked up my phone quickly and there it was. My very first customer lead! I couldn't believe it. My attention veered away from the speaker and onto contacting the lead. I phoned them without having any idea what to say. An elderly gentleman picked up and I told him I had received his message that he was looking for a structural engineer to inspect his residence. I quickly offered to come over to his residence right away without realizing I had no tools (not even a flashlight), measuring tape or anything. I am sure you can remember how it felt the moment you landed your first customer. You feel like you're on Cloud Nine, on top of the world. You have the "I can do it" attitude. Nothing in the world matters anymore because you can see the light!

When I got to his residence, I began to realize that I was not ready to do an inspection. Without a tape or a flashlight, all I could do was walk around and observe to the extent of my abilities. The owner provided me with the tools I needed, which at the time seemed harmless but as you will soon see, actually built a sense of animosity towards me. When I was done, I told the homeowner I would work on the report and have it to him the following week. I literally had no templates. At my college, we called it "Learn By Doing." That is exactly what I was doing. When

I first drafted the letter it was very extensive, detailed, and addressed all aspects of his residence which I felt were important. After I sent the initial report, I sighed with relief and felt a sense of accomplishment. I did it, I told myself.

Within a few days, he responded with an extensive list of questions. (Note, my fee for the work was fixed, and not based on how much time I actually spent on the visit and on his particular project). His email was long and it took me some time to respond. He was critical, lacking anything positive to say, and was contrary by nature. I replied shortly thereafter and made some revisions to my initial report. Once again, I did not charge for my additional time. He wrote back with some additional requests. I followed up once again.

This continued until one day I was in the financial district of San Francisco. During this time, I worked an eight-to-five job to pay my bills while working on this new side hustle. I won't ever forget crossing the street and seeing an email that I had just received my first review. I anxiously opened the email while paying no attention to walking in the middle of a busy intersection. In business, we sometimes drop what we are doing, and focus on the item on hand. The problem with this is we lose focus on everything and everyone around us. In this case, I saw something that changed me forever. I saw a one-star review. My heart dropped, I started sweating, fear kicked in and I screamed inside. "Humza, what were you thinking?" I thought to myself. "You thought you could be an entrepreneur? Just stick to what you know. What will happen next? Is he going to sue me?" How many times has something happened and you were immediately launched into fear mode? I thought all customers were good customers, right? The review was anything but positive; he ripped everything I did and called me out for not having the tools when I showed up. He was similar to millions of other customers who choose to express their dissatisfaction by writing negative reviews. No matter how many times I responded, replied, and revised, there was no way to turn an unhappy person into a Happy Customer. I spent countless hours trying to satisfy someone who had no intention or desire to be satisfied. I disregarded and discounted my services for the sake and well-being of somebody else. That was all because I was putting the customer first.

Turning a negative into a positive

At the time, I did not realize that there were several other customers out there, waiting to find someone like me. How many times have you had a bad experience with a customer and decided that this was your last straw? How many times did you decide to quit your business because you were so emotionally drained from trying to please your customers?

Well, I sure have, and it is part of the building process. Based on just one review, I wanted to put an end to everything. Is that the right thing to do? No. But it sure is the easy thing to do. Often, we focus our energy on trying to meet our clients' expectations, and we forget our own unique purpose. However, it is we who created those expectations when we sold ourselves to that customer. By setting unrealistic expectations from the start, it is easy to overcommit and make it impossible to deliver.

Focus on the low hanging fruit first

You must become a millionaire before you can become a billionaire. Steve Jobs said not to do something with the intention to make loads of money but do something with the intention of providing people with the next great thing. Offer them a product they themselves couldn't have thought of getting used to. That was how he achieved the success that he did. Make your business your focus and treat it like a baby; nurture it, teach it, and let it grow naturally.

I could have taken the easy route and let my customers shut my business before it even started. Many customers have that effect on us, and we go along with that feeling and lose faith in our business before we even have an opportunity to develop it. Even the most successful companies have failed, let down consumers, but their resilience kept them afloat.

TIME TO 'FIRE' YOUR CUSTOMERS

Walt Disney was thrown out of a creative agency for not being creative enough. He did not allow that to hold him back from doing what he wanted, and he ended up making arguably the most famous production studio in the world. This is what your focus should be. Find something you are passionate about and just focus on it. When we are passionate about our business, others will take notice and as time progresses, the right customers will actually find you.

Chapter 3

Review or be Reviewed

We have all heard the phrase, "Customers come first." How many of us have fallen victim to the "customers first" mentality? Customers are important and a necessity, but not at the cost of your actual business. While serving customers is one of the goals for a business, serving the right customers is how a business can grow.

Going after customers similar to my first customer is a bad idea. I admit I was not well prepared, but had I turned down the excitement of my first customer and possible revenue I could have taken better notice of the cues.

When it comes to serving customers, businesses in general try to satisfy and give a good customer experience overall. As an entrepreneur, your time is very precious.

TIME TO 'FIRE' YOUR CUSTOMERS

There are only twenty-four hours in a day and that is not changing anytime soon. By focusing on customers in general and not certain customers, you miss countless opportunities. Why focus on a fallen rotten fruit when you have a tree full of ripe ones? The key here is to find customers who will add *value* to your business. They all bring some level of revenue. How can you find value-based customers? Firstly, by word of mouth. When you invest your time and money on those who are as enthusiastic about your product as you are, they will not only come back, but will also bring in more people to try out your brand. Value-based customers are willing to pay more money when they understand your product or service. They understand your business differentiators and do not view you as a commodity. Secondly, good reviews. A valuable customer will give it back to you in terms of positive feedback. They will share their experience which will validate your business online.

In this age of social media, where information spreads within minutes and seconds, a good customer review goes a long way. Take a moment and make a list of customers who if called upon would write you a review. Use the following script:

"Hi, this is Humza from Acme, Inc. I'm calling today because we wanted to reach out to a select few of our preferred customers. We had the opportunity to work together and currently we are undergoing a community outreach and thought about you. Could I count on you to share your experience with our company for online viewers to read about?"

You can also incentivize; however, this usually is not necessary for these customers. They value your business and understand that by writing a review they may help alleviate concerns people may commonly have regarding your business.

If you are shopping online at Amazon for example, you will rely solely on the reviews written by people who purchased the product(s) you're considering.

As you read on, you'll begin to recognize many challenges that you face today with your customers or your business. And not only that, but you will become better equipped to handle those challenges in the form of customers, branding, marketing etc.

In the world today, with a lot of startups emerging, you might have wondered how you can stand out. One answer to this is that you need to be as smart as your customer. Do not underestimate the degree to which their knowledge of what is out there in the market gives them power. Just because you love your product/service, doesn't mean everyone else will too. Now how do you act smart? In today's world we are all facing a variety of challenges and the one who caters to these, wins. Simple. In essence, your business must solve a problem.

Businesses solve problems

Dandelion is a startup in the energy industry. The owner of Dandelion knows that climate change is becoming the most talked-about topic in the world. Their business involves the installation of geothermal pumps as affordable as rooftop solar. The goal is to harness energy from the earth's surface, which allows homes to stay hot and cold respectively during different seasons. This reduces carbon emissions from heating and cooling. Buildings in the US account for 39% of carbon emissions, so by installing these pumps at the time of construction Dandelion has put the customers at ease about their potential contribution to the problem of carbon emissions.

Discover Customer Whys

Finding the right customer is sometimes about knowing their whys. Why should they work with you and care about your business? Because you think they should? Remember, people in general worry about themselves, not others' businesses. Ultimately the objective should involve a combination of two things. Creating value and impact to their specific needs. I always screen my customers for pains, headaches, issues, desires, and wants, and focus my sales approach on resolving those same items. I help them envision the experience from the start until the end. People want to be in the know and have some control of the outcome. Keeping customers in the dark will always lead to a dead end.

Do you have a cat? Or any other pet for that matter? Chances are you have or have had a pet. The same is the case with many of your customers. They not only own a pet, but would do anything, I repeat, ANYTHING for that cat, dog or pet. So why not love their pet(s) the same way? Well, Footloose did. Not only does it manufacture a litter box that can clean itself, it monitors the health of the pet and reports it to the owner through a mobile app. How convenient, right?

These are just two examples to help you to understand the importance of grasping the underlying concerns of various customers and how these can be tackled. It doesn't matter if your startup category is not the same as Dandelion's or Footloose's. All that matters is how you cater to your customer and make your product/service solve their problems.

Chapter 4

Traits and Types of Customers

The following are the types of customers:

(A rating of 10 is the most desirable, and a 1 is the worst for your business)

The Frugal Customer: This customer focuses more on costs than value. Normally you can identify this culprit by paying attention to the clues they drop. Often, they start, remind, and end with words that are cost sensitive. They ignore all the talking points about what makes you so great, unique, special, and just want to know one thing:

What does it cost? Run fast and never look back from these customers.

Score: 3 The frugal customer will cost you more in the short and long runs. Since they are driven by cost and not value, it puts additional pressure on your business to deliver results. At a time when freelancing is at an all-time high, this may be a good building block at the start of a business. However, desperate times call for desperate measures. In some cases, depending on the circumstances you may need some of these customers to ride a slow wave. Otherwise stay far away.

The Baggage Customer: This customer comes to you usually with some baggage from a previous encounter or experience. They lay out their previous experience and frustrations and expect you to be their savior and save their day. Most of the time you will get a sense that they play the victim card by only focusing on what they do not have. You may need to dig deep and ask questions like, "What would you have done differently to create a more desirable outcome?" Get comfortable knowing that this customer may question everything you say or do, which will require more of your time. Expect a surcharge due to the baggage.

Score: 5 This customer has gone through an experience to understand partially what you may or may not offer. Treat them like a boxer in a boxing match. They have already been through a few rounds and may be bruised up. Since you are in Round 4 with them, try to steer the conversation by focusing on realistic expectations that you are comfortable with and can deliver on. You can also jab at them with an upcharge by letting them know that you are a premium service. Focus on delivering off of their pains.

The Annoying Customer: This customer is easy to spot. They call you and text you constantly without any regard for your time. You may receive late night correspondence, or repeated phone calls throughout the day. They are determined to track you and make you drop what you are doing. Like the baggage customer, they may question you each step of the way, so be prepared to spend extra time dealing with their annoyance.

Score: 2 Annoying customers drag down not only your time but your business. They will find you by stalking you in multiple ways until you give them the attention they crave. Since they are rarely happy or content, they will continue to annoy you until they can find someone else to annoy. Good luck if you decided to take one on. You will probably be eager to be done with them quickly.

The Happy Customer: This customer contacts you with a positive and excited tone of voice. They generally thank you for your time and appreciate your attentiveness to their request(s). They ask questions about things outside of business and possibly even ask about your personal life. They show general care and well-being. In most cases, this customer will provide positive feedback even if it is with constructive criticism. The Happy Customer does care about value, unlike the frugal customer, however they may still be cost-sensitive. Providing happiness does cost money, but this happy customer will be your forever customer assuming you follow through with your promises.

Score: 8 Happy customers tend to make you do your best, normally they speak well of you, even if there were some bumps in the road. You tend to go the extra mile to keep them in their positive spirits. Happy customers tend to raise your and employees' morale.

The Cool Customer: This customer tends to be friendly, cracks jokes, listens and does not interrupt. One unique feature about this customer is they tend to carry on conversations on topics beyond business. You can get friendly with this customer, which will give your personal WHY power (internal motivation) while working with them. They usually do not worry, just contact you and then wait around and let you steer the boat.

Score: 8 Cool customers tend to be sociable and will promote your business when given the opportunity. They are always sensitive to your schedule and try not to overburden you. In addition, they understand costs, add-ons etc. and are easy to talk to.

The "You Owe Me Customer": This customer thinks that you work for them. The moment they hired you and gave you some money they want to be in control. Their personalities can be intimidating, overwhelming and lead to panic. They request changes to your standard contracts and demand you make their project your priority.

Score 6 These customers are red flags from the start. By requesting changes to your contract, they transmit how they like to be in control and set the conditions. Since they expect a lot from your business, make sure you budget for their high expectations.

However, for a new business, this sense of being on your A-game game can help you refine some of your processes and techniques. This customer can make your business better in some circumstances.

The Freeloader Customer: This customer comes off as a hybrid between annoying and frugal. They demand free work from the business at every opportunity. Sometimes you can discover them early on in the process when they mention a discount prior to signing on with your business. The problem is once you give them a freebie their requests only become more frequent. They can also be threatening if you do not agree with their demands. Proceed with massive caution.

Score 0 These customers are reasons why business owners go out of business. Freeloading not only steals revenue from the business but ultimately can end the actual business. Under no circumstances should this customer be affiliated with your business. If you had the unfortunate luck of working with one of these, you most likely wanted to turn off the lights to your business.

The PERFECT Customer: This type of customer is rare. By understanding the qualities of a perfect customer, you will quickly be able to sort out clientele and focus on surrounding yourself with only the perfect customers. A perfect customer is essentially a combination of most of the previously described customers. They are a mix of cool, happy, annoying, baggage and frugal. You might ask why I would want a customer who has baggage or is annoying or frugal. When these qualities are the sole qualities of the customer, they tend to be very undesirable. However, if these qualities are understood properly, you can use them to achieve more desirable outcome. Keep in mind, a "frugal" or "annoying" customer may appear initially as a happy or cool customer, however as the surface erodes and you're doing business with this individual, other sides may begin to show. I have several annoying, frugal, cool and happy customers. The perfect customer may initially be happy, but quickly become annoyed when there are added costs (frugal kicks in), lack of communication (annoyance kicks in), or lack of progress (baggage kicks in). In short, a client who is a mixture of all these qualities will in turn keep you on your "A" game and give you ways to improve rather than self-destruct. Your business will become more successful rather than more stressful. Business relationships become positive synergy.

You may also want to look after the **LOYAL customers**. These are the customers who make up just a small fraction of the consumer base but keeping them happy will generate the maximum return on your investment in them. They will say good things about you, which is extremely essential for your business, as it is free publicity. Following up with them is essential to you and your customer-building relationship. Keep them happy and they will keep you happy.

Another set of customers that is critical to your business is the **impulsive customers**, or better described as **bonus** customers. Why are they important? Simply because it's easy to grab their attention and get them to buy your product or service even when they do not necessarily need it. They will buy whatever comes their way as long as it makes sense to them at that very moment. It needs to be out there, attractive, easy-to-use and just simply a form of shortcut or benefit.

Chapter 5

Drawbacks of Being Entirely Customer-Centric

All too often we are told from a young age that it's "customers first." However, even the most successful businesses do not thrive without the dedication and sacrifice of their employees. At the root of every successful business is a culture, a why, a desire to deliver results to their customers. These results are only made by possible with extraordinary effort by the employees. In the following chapter, we look at some of the drawbacks of being a customer-centric business and the effects it may have.

1) Loss of business essence

Firstly, once you commit to your customers alone, not only does your business lose its own essence that reflects through its organizational culture, but the business becomes bent upon ONLY producing that which is required by the customer. It also means enhancing the customer's experience with every purchase/consumption and that can be quite a task. For your business, this could potentially lead to a loss, but also removes your focus from establishing the business into serving with greater purpose.

2) Pleasing the customer can be costly

Secondly, let's be honest: the amount of money you will have to spend on grabbing your customer's attention is going to be enormous. You may have the perfect, most desirable product ready for your target customer, but if you don't advertise it through every effective means, it will be of no use. Whereas, if you put in some effort and invest in your employees and build a work environment that best suits them, the results will be far more favorable and go a long way. These emotionally and physically invested employees will bring the customers to buy your product, without any additional cost!

If you want happy clients at the end of the day, you need to make sure your internal work environment is happy. Once you have those emotionally invested employees, prompting the customers to buy the product/service of your brand, you have everything you need. Not only strong external clients, but unbreakable, valuable relationships with your employees and your organization. More light will be shed upon this concept as you go further into this book.

When you aim to become more customer-centric, just claiming it will not be enough. When companies claim they are customer-centric, few actually live up to their word and implement the strategies required to run a customer-driven company. For example, it is not just the job of the marketing department to hold on to the customers and conduct research to keep customers loyal to your brand. The entire organization needs to come together and form a culture that works best for customer-centricity. In order to run your business in a consistent and profitable manner, you need to involve all spheres of your business.

Do you really want to go through this hassle of simply pleasing your customer only? Your business in its initial stage requires your full attention like a newborn baby does. You must be on your toes, and that precious time and effort should go into doing and producing something long-term and solid. Put all your energy into recognizing the right customers for your business and make them the focus. Building valuable relationships with them is what you will need to focus on and that will benefit your business in the long run.

Real Story:

A while back, I had a client who was a couple. They came into my office one day and discussed their upcoming project. They wanted to expand their residence into a two-story and needed design, engineering and construction services. The couple came off as very friendly, easy to work with, and shortly thereafter signed our contract to proceed with our design services. During the design and engineering phase, the couple seemed easygoing, and looking back at it I would compare it to dating. When you work out of an office and see a client once a month, they appear happy, easygoing, satisfied. However, would they be the exact same way if you were married to them? We would later find that out in the construction phase, when you see them every day.

When we first provided a bid for the entire project, we were told that the budget was too high and that the client would prefer to do some of the work on his own. Now he was no Bob Villa, so the red flag went up when he made the request and followed it by requesting us to help him along the way. He did not offer to compensate us for that time, but rather made it sound like a small favor. At the same time the husband was losing his patience with the city and began sending passive aggressive emails to the planning department. I ignored these red flags, due to the excitement I felt anticipating building his project.

Shortly after he got his permit, he expected us to drop what we were doing and begin his project right away. He looked solely thru his own lens and not thru the company's, with no consideration of what other projects we may have had on our schedule. It was only his project that mattered. It was soon after we began that we realized we did not have the staff to support his project. In addition, his wife would curse out the staff and soon it became apparent we were dealing with an annoying client. I was at the mall one Friday night with my family when I got a text from the couple demanding immediate action. Instead of spending time with my loved ones I scrambled to call our project manager and devise a plan to keep them "happy." The problem with this approach was I neglected the organic nature of construction and the business, and instead tried to control the inevitable. At one point during the project, the client had his father-in-law fly in from out of town to assist with the project. Due to some complications during the project, his father-in-law was forced to have to come back later. Out of my own goodwill, I offered to pay for his ticket. To my surprise the client did not even acknowledge my offer. It was $1,200 out of my pocket in my naïve attempt to turn an unhappy person into a happy customer. To top it all off, I found out the client was trying to hire our staff to work for him. Ignoring the red flags along the way, I was set up for failure and the project turned out worse because I had tried to be customer-centric and focus on their happiness. We ended up battling our differences through meditation and although it took some back and forth, it ultimately was ruled in my favor. I live my life with principle, and I knew our firm had done nothing wrong. However, I will not let terrible customers change my principles and fundamental business ethics, which are transparency and honesty.

Chapter 6

Not all money is good money (Choosing between $ and Intuition)

The whole world has money. Money is like love, there is an infinite amount of it.

At least, that is what I believe. If you want more, you must earn it. When choosing your customers, selling to ten wrong customers is less valuable than selling to one right customer. That one right customer may be able to provide more business for you in the future than ten wrong customers. Taking a slow road to money does not hurt you because at the end you will get to your desired destination.

You can usually get a sense of who a customer is from the initial encounter. If during the initial encounter you sense that the customer may not be your ideal customer, follow your intuition with follow up questions. How much time and effort do you want to waste with the wrong customer? It's to your benefit to instead focus your time on the right folks who want to be a part of your fan club.

EXAMPLE: The Naïve Customer

We received a call from someone who just inherited their parents' home and decided to remodel with dollars they also inherited. Their idea was to move in and make the residence their dream home. From discussing the project with the prospect, it became apparent that the person was naïve about the expenses they would be facing. We reviewed their plans and realized that they would need to give up many of their ideas to make their unrealistic budget work. This was immediately met with a tone of disappointment from the customer. Realizing that this was already an unhappy and unrealistic customer, it was time to move on. If we attempted to drag out the relationship, we would start off on the wrong foot, never meet their expectations, and play catch up the entire time. Although we would have made revenue in our initial design and engineering work, it would have dragged out the unrealistic expectation and now in the middle of the date you're breaking up. You wasted time and money, two things that are very precious to most people. Being up front, honest, and transparent can help you to avoid customers who try to put their unrealistic expectations on to you.

The reality is the client will find themselves making more and more sacrifices and becoming more and more disappointed. As a result, they will not be the type of client that will bring in referrals and will most likely write a bad review as well. When a business has enough bad reviews echoing the same complaint, readers begin to believe what they are reading. Say goodbye to future clients! Here you should forgo the instant gratification of money and follow your intuition.

Chapter 7

Your engine: Employees

Today more than ever, we live in booming economy where unemployment is at an all-time low. Although at the time of writing this book, the covid-19 coronavirus has struck and the economy is tanking due to this new reality we are facing, excluding outside factors out of our control, the economy is doing relatively well. In any business, unless you a solopreneur, the way to grow your business and vision is by finding those who are willing and eager to spread your message. Now, I know some of you are thinking that your job does not give you the cell phone of your CEO, however most businesses are small businesses. When starting or developing a new business, finding key talent will ultimately lay the blueprint for how successful your business will be. If you still are not on the employees-first bandwagon, then ask yourself this: Imagine if you had the world's number-one product – something that everybody wanted, needed and a must-have. When people called up the phone number to order the product they were greeted by rude, standoffish customer service reps who did not care about your business. How many potential customers would you lose? How many of those customers would tell their friends, family, and essentially potential customers about your terrible customer service? No matter how successful your company is, the employees are the engine that makes it run. Without them, the business would be mismanaged and ultimately shut down.

Remember the work force behind all your operations and learn how to value them fully. Your employees are the ones cranking away, and if you are in a service business their time is billable which translates to revenue for you. Just as you need to service your car and keep the engine in good condition, pay attention to your employee s' well-being. Here's an example of where you should pay attention: An employee is assigned to a client who is causing them a lot of grief, making them work extended hours, troubleshooting nitpicky complaints. They are doing their best to please the customer on behalf of the business, but at the same time engines eventually burn out when they are not well maintained. This could result in a poor performance not only for this annoying customer but also for other good customers. An employee's morale shall not be overlooked. If you bring in enough bad customers, they will not only take a toll on you, but your employees and entire business. Once the environment is full of toxic customers, it will be very difficult to get employees excited again.

Employers need to be aware and maintain an open communication with their employees so that management is made aware of uncomfortable situations and can intervene on behalf of the employee. This could be a situation where you fire your client in order to save your employee. Imagine the gratitude an employee could have if their employer fights for them. Talk about potential for some serious loyalty.

Chapter 8

Being selective

In this chapter, we will focus on criteria and sample questions for one to answer when choosing to work with a client.

An example to use when working with a customer is to understand what is important to them. Find out what their internal "Why" is, and by understanding and taking note, you may have a better shot at earning their trust.

Sample questionnaire for Clients:

List the most important and least important factors starting with the most important:

1. Stay within budget
2. Stay on schedule and finish on time

3. Cost
4. Quality of work
5. Communication
6. Accessibility
7. Responsiveness
8. Skills and knowledge

Since we want to focus on value-based clients and not so much cost-conscious clients, try to discuss some case studies on how ultimately your business was the right business for the job. Focus on competitor differentiators if your client feels your business is a commodity (which most are). Value-based clients seek more than the actual commodity when choosing a business to work with. They normally have done some level of research so don't hesitate to ask what they know about your business. If they found you on an online database such as Yelp, they only understand how many stars your business is worth. If you to want your customers to believe in your business, you will have to believe it in as well. If a prospective client calls you and you can tell that this customer will not be part of your ideal base, be honest. Say something like, "I appreciate the call, however based on your needs I feel like we may not be the best fit for you at this time." You can show the client that their interests are important to you and if you can, point them toward another provider. If you have done that much, you have not only alleviated yourself from taking on this customer, but you also solved their problem.

Being selective does not simply translate to telling people no. Telling people no will not make you a better business leader. Saying no without any follow-up lets the customer know that they're not important enough for you. Their friends and family will most likely hear about their personal experience when looking for a business like yours. I will say it again: do not hurt your business by simply saying no. Be upfront and honest while still maintaining a level of professionalism.

Businesses are built on the ability to deliver on promises and the reputation of those who run the actual business.

Chapter 9

Fire Bad, Hire Good Customers

Have you ever wondered if there was a way out? I mean beyond shutting down your actual business. Sometimes we settle for the reality and make this our new reality. We continue to allow our customers drive our businesses and we simply watch this from the sidelines. My hope is to ensure that this book helps you watch your business from 30,000 feet above to help it grow. What does it look like from up there? What are some of the things you are paying attention to that were not so apparent from the sidelines? This is done in

TIME TO 'FIRE' YOUR CUSTOMERS

sports, for a good reason; we watch the game using several camera angles. This is because in order to see the entire game and get the best experience, we need to view it from several angles to capture the entire game.

The same applies to your business. Instead of sitting on the sidelines, view it from several angles. If you choose to stay on the sidelines, just watch your customers take your business away. What would happen if you took yourself out of your business for a week? Would it fail or would it continue to run? Are you a business owner or an entrepreneur?

A business owner works inside his/her business while an entrepreneur provides a working system that at its highest efficiency allows him or her to step away and watch the business thrive. The problem today is understanding where the business is, and where does it need to be to give you that freedom. There are things in life we can control: customer selection, the types of people we hire, office locations, type of equipment, etc. There are many things in life we cannot control, like weather, traffic, natural disasters, people, etc.

Let go of the things which do not have a net effect on your business. Unless you are in a transportation business, traffic will hardly have any effect on you outside of work commuting. Living in the bay area, I have adjusted my schedule to get up and leave my house by 6:00 a.m. to beat the morning traffic. That gives me full control of my time, how to start my day, and I can get ahead before the world wakes up and tries to take my time. All problems have solutions, but you must acknowledge, confront, understand, and address. No excuses.

Having bad customers can easily become a habit, so much that you fail to recognize all the red flags when choosing to work with them.

Prioritize yourself and your business above everything else. The positives need to outweigh the negatives. A leader must be comfortable with making difficult decisions. You are not a leader if you let your customers drive your business. Once you have checked out of a business, this usually becomes the end result. You let your customers and staff down, but more importantly you let yourself down. Don't cheat yourself, stay positive, keep a firm grasp on what you can control and focus on getting rid of the bad to make room for the good.

Imagine how much energy a bad customer takes. You listen to constant complaints, disappointment, problem after problem. At what point would you realize that this unhappy person will not magically transform into a Happy Customer? Your purpose in business is not to satisfy but to gratify. Be thankful for health, dedicated employees, good customers and loved ones. Seek gratitude in what you do, and you will naturally repel bad customers. By understanding and accepting the reality that not all customers are good customers, then can you begin to transform yourself and your business into letting go of those fewer desirable clients and focusing on the clients who clearly are your biggest fans. Try not to fear the future, remember to focus on today, and not tomorrow. Who would have ever predicted that in 2020 all this has already happened? We lost the biggest basketball legend of all time and now the world has shut down due to the spread of a virus. How much of any of that was in your control? Many businesses are shutting down, employees are losing work, everybody is worried. Can you stop the inevitable? Let nature take its course and begin to realign your efforts on what type of customers are ideal for your business. Just like most things in life, no health, dental, vision plan caters to everybody. While some people are extremely healthy and rarely need to see a doctor, others may not be so fortunate and need constant visits. Focus your business on establishing a solid culture with meaning. Get your employees as excited as you were when you first started and remain the captain without making others feel like you are. I understand people need leaders, but leaders are not necessarily dictators.

Sit down and perform the following exercise with your staff. Ask them to reflect on the customers they have served or worked with and ask them to list the qualities and traits of each customer. Compare notes and see if you find similarities. Start to develop a strategy which can be easily implemented once you have a clear picture of what your ideal customer looks like. Do they earn a certain income? Is your business catering to a certain age group? Do not discriminate under any circumstances – this is an exercise to discover your ideal customer base. I can guarantee your ideal customers have similarities across the board. Were they price conscious? Did they complain or nag throughout the process? Did they follow up with gratitude?

Once you are sure of yourself and your business, you will realize that you will never be able to satisfy a client based on constant complaints and disappointment. It is time to let go. As they are expressing their disappointment, complaints, problems, simply offer to take a step back and open the door for them to look elsewhere. You can offer them a refund, partial refund and suggest another company that might suit them better. Take the emotions out of all of this; be objective. By accepting that you are not a good fit and directing them to another option, you have alleviated the burden. At this point they will either realize they have gone overboard with their complaints or simply move on. Either way it is a win-win. I have built my businesses and fundamentals with that principal in mind. Both sides must win for it to work. Not just for today but for the long term as well. You are in control, give it your 100% and never look back.

Chapter 10

Off to the races!

Now we know that not all customers are good customers, and we must focus on our ideal base, let's get started. Recall that great customers will ultimately be your strongest asset. Beyond referrals and great online reviews, they will help grow your business organically.

A good customer will care about more than just themselves. I have had several customers over the years check in, ask questions about the general health and nature of my business. They were not asking about how much money we make, but more like compliments to the staff, the enjoyment they had working with our team, our office environment, and many times their referrals.

Some of you may be feeling stuck with your current customers, but starting today make it a point to evaluate your strategies for acquiring new customers. If a customer cannot deliver the values, we invest our time into, reconsider your relationship.

Three core values that show we are in the race competing for this customer:

1. Value based
2. Gratitude not attitude
3. Referral network

Value-based customers are willing to pay more than frugal customers. They are thankful and offer themselves for referrals. If you could take a moment and write down at least five to ten customers who may fit the bill. Reach out to them in the next one or two days and send a simple check-in email.

"Dear Humza,

I hope all is well with you. You may recall that we worked on the ACME project together. I want to use this medium to appreciate you for doing business with us; our company enjoyed being the right resource for your project. Hope all is well with you and your family. Cheers."

Emails like the above that are simple and straight to the point don't seem like you're asking or demanding anything. You want to start off with a simple intro not a sales request. If you sound salesy you will eventually be tuned out. If the customer replies, then you can proceed with asking if they know of anyone who you could help out.

TIME TO 'FIRE' YOUR CUSTOMERS

I recall a woman who came to an open house when I first became a real estate agent. She was very standoffish, criticized the home, and did not have a friendly attitude. If you had asked me to list the buyers who I thought would buy the home, she would be dead last for sure. Well guess what? After the open house, she was the first one to call me and request to make an offer for the home. The first thing she noted was I was not salesy at all and she appreciated that. Sometimes your customers are the baggage customers. You can identify them, stay true to who you are, and let them repel or be attracted to you. No harm no foul.

You are the product of the five people you surround yourself with. If you have a great customer, they most likely have great referrals. Cold calling and trying to make sales is something most people are not designed to do. Being natural, organic, transparent and to the point is authentic. When sending emails like the one above lets your good customers see that you genuinely care about them, you will remain on top of mind for that product or service which you offer.

For those who are completely new to the business world, try experimenting with friends and family. Show gratitude and thanks for past experiences and let them know you genuinely care.

I hope that with some of the ideas, thoughts, and suggestions throughout this book you are now ready to fire and hire the right customers for your business. We all strive for a higher meaning and purpose in life – which gets lost when we focus our energies on the wrong things. Take action immediately by identifying the traits of your ideal customer, give thanks to them, and grow your referral network. Request reviews from happy customers and let them know you appreciate them. Remember birthdays, anniversaries and take your customer service skills up a few notches. You got this, let's go!

www.ingramcontent.com/pod-product-compliance
Lightning Source LLC
Chambersburg PA
CBHW071123240526
45465CB00023B/796